T0207912

A Walk of
Many Paths

David Ferguson

authorHOUSE®

AuthorHouse™
1663 Liberty Drive
Bloomington, IN 47403
www.authorhouse.com
Phone: 1 (800) 839-8640

© 2015 David Ferguson. All rights reserved.

Be sure to check out my website to find out more about my poetry and
where it comes from: http://www.awalkofmanypaths.com/

No part of this book may be reproduced, stored in a retrieval system, or
transmitted by any means without the written permission of the author.

Published by AuthorHouse   12/16/2015

ISBN: 978-1-5049-6889-8 (sc)
ISBN: 978-1-5049-6888-1 (e)

Library of Congress Control Number: 2015920994

Print information available on the last page.

Any people depicted in stock imagery provided by Thinkstock are models,
and such images are being used for illustrative purposes only.
Certain stock imagery © Thinkstock.

This book is printed on acid-free paper.

Because of the dynamic nature of the Internet, any web addresses or links contained in
this book may have changed since publication and may no longer be valid. The views
expressed in this work are solely those of the author and do not necessarily reflect the
views of the publisher, and the publisher hereby disclaims any responsibility for them.

DEDICATION

———

For those who have experienced the horrors of the
reality of the Foster Care system and to those who
had to learn to survive completely on their own.

"I learned that courage was not the absence of fear, but the triumph over it. The brave man is not he who does not feel afraid, but he who conquers that fear."
— <u>Nelson Mandela</u>

Contents

Part One

Era of the Troubled One

Utopian Family

Celebrations come alive, as the first is bred.
Flames of fatherhood ignite within,
while the strings of motherhood are implanted.
The smoker's tendency leeches his child's air,
for he is born without breath,
so yet another creature is birthed this day.

It screams the devil's insanity.
Foster summons the authority of placement.
The child is stolen in the mental's eyes,
though witnesses would say otherwise.
Within the flawless family mirror,
a tiny crack appears unveiling dysfunction.

5 years have passed in the second realm,
where chances are given away like prizes.
Family returns to the original state of being,
though uncertainty festers in the beast's domain,
when the Utopia will be consumed by 666.
It will become the ill-omen of deterioration.

Positivity dissipates and fades into emptiness.
Voids are crammed with fiery negativity.
Delirious calmness plagues our atmosphere.
Thunder strikes home with ferocity.
Fear evolves from safety's offspring,
now the demons of hell are unleashed.

Crows & Ravens

Bad luck shadows these black birds,
as they are known as tricksters.
Their speech sounds like death to mortals.
Their presence radiates misunderstood evil.
How many chances can life make with mine?

Cursed I am within this concealing room.
Fight or flights are my odds.
My wings are clipped, so flight is pointless.
Dubbed I am as the fighter of freedom.
Locked I am in a steel cage.

Delirium ripples into my sanity.
Fear burrows deeper into my delicate soul.
Anger sparks flames in my gentle heart.
Sadness claws at my blackened pupils.
Hunger awakens deep within.

I peck, I claw, I snap at the lock.
I screech a forgotten dialect.
My voice is simply voiceless.
Carelessly food is tossed in.
Water rains from the sky.

One hand unlocks it.
I strike, blood trickles.
I claw; I struggle to obtain freedom's scent.
I hop; I hop from oppression's gate.
Never am I to return to the devil's domain.

Purity

United we stand as clear slates.
We are all born of divine states.
First Sages of late introduces insanity,
while environments dance with our bodies,
and sacred water claims to clear the soul.

Impurities leaks into our essence,
after birth sanities becomes casualties.
Distractions sprout at every turn,
and obsessions spark their own lives.
Together we lose ourselves in a field of rapid-fire.

Wars erupt between the savage ones.
Impurities are pure, and purities are impure.
Lead by confusing screeches of religious drones.
Left, right, and center believes in Right.
What is rightness compared to happiness?

Acceptance is the forbidden word.
Survivors long for the resounding recognition.
Calmness is the only gateway to peace.
Its only golden key is the power to let go.
Release the seal of anger and judgement.

Reality

Do you find life as being a grim ordeal?
Do dreams determine your deserved fate?
Are these trials nightmares or is it real'?

Events honest or true are often surreal.
Dreams are fantasies for us at any rate.
Do you find life as being a grim ordeal?

Hardships can silence you, so learn to feel.
Challenging the tricks and lies will sedate.
Are these trials nightmares or is it real?

Face your fears head on, so do not keel.
Have a strong might, and darkness will deflate.
Do you find life as being a grim ordeal?

Shine bright and the darkness will squeal.
Forget to forgive and one will learn hate.
Are these trials nightmares or is it real?

It really does not bode well for those who seal.
Cutting yourself off from the truth is not great.
Do you find life as being a grim ordeal?

Keeping your shields high makes life very unreal.
People with similar issues can relate.
Do you find life as being a grim ordeal?
Are these trials nightmares or is it real?

Origins
Part I

_____

I wander into the house of shadows, of smoke, of mirrors,
where the air I breathe is a poisonous fume.
Every, breath I take leaves scars in my lungs.
Towers of platters, mugs, and silverware
surround the house left unclean.

Everywhere, there is dirt, insects, and sticky spills.
It reeks of the rotten foods, undone laundry,
and the ashes of the previously smoked smoke.
In the center lies a beast lying on his thrown of indolence.
His maid tends to his every need.

His maid is the factory of his addictions,
and the supplier of his issues.
Dark energies emanate from this dark abyss.
Stained curtains clog the brightness of outdoors.
Air is trapped by closed windows.
Old newspapers litter the floors.

Emotions are stirred.

The beast is aggravated.

The maid is tortured by the beast's illusive behaviour.

The gremlins run in fear after the maid is tossed.

The maid follows them.

Locked they are in a room holding each other.

Hoping, wishing, and praying the dark entity leaves.

The beast rushes into the open, shirtless.

His anger spreads like wildfire.

To me this is the place of hell.

Origins Part II
Awakening of the Beast

———

I awaken from my slumber.
The day was like every other.
Yet my surroundings were unusually calm.
The clouds were assembling.
Energies began its polluted dance.

I wander into the plume of black smoke.
The putrid scent of the beast is rampant.
Nearly I faint of another scent next door.
Gasping like a fish out of water.
It was like breathing in sewage gas.

I stumble into the room of relief,
which was filled with pubic hairs
bundled up like balls of wool
rolling across the tiled floor
Stained and encrusted with a deeply yellow substance.

I am relieved, but I timidly exit the room.
Careful to be as silent as the grave.
I could hear the motor of the sleeping beast.
I could see his unclean, unshaven face.
Swiftly, I run across to the winding stairs.

Vigilantly, I peer around the railing,
into the lion's den only to see emptiness.
It reeked of the previously smoked smokes.
Sticky spills encrusted the table in the centre.
Dirt stained the fabric sofa, rugs, and walls.

I dash into the kitchen of bareness.
The sink, full of unsanitary dishes.
Dirt consumes the window too.
Coffee stains those ugly curtains, I must add.
I climb on the contaminated counter.

Yes! I have found a clean glass; I say in earnest.
As I open the fridge, another putrid odor burst.
Something had expired.
Maybe it was the cheese... the yogurt.
Thankfully, it wasn't the milk.

I poured the remaining bit...not much.
It tasted smooth and satisfying.
As I close the door, I noticed something.
The roar of the chainsaw stopped.
It had awakened, and so shall everything else.

The little gnome staggers down.
The unwise elf stumbles.
The beast grumbles.
The coffee pot rumbles.
Sleep clings to the trio.

It has awoken, so the games begin.
Eyes of the beast widen.
Evil now lives within.
His deranged mind engulfs the light.
Fear replaces all serenity.

It has a hold of my feet, so I dangle.
I am dropped, so I scream.
Bang, I am shot.
I flee into the room of security.
I hear another thud.

Frantic feet rush up the stairs.
The door flies open,
The fearful creatures rush in.
The door flies shut, and is locked.
More thuds rip through the beast's domain.

A final slam of the front door,
stops our hearts.
Tears stream like rivers.
Breathing is heavy.
We hold each other, wondering why.

Cracks are now deep within.
The flame of fatherhood is extinguished.
Strings of motherhood are severed.
Independence is now greatly sought.
Any remnants of love or laughter are erased.
Family begins to drift apart.

Cops are notified of the beast's actions.
He is described as being shirtless.
Dark energies spread to the outside world.
Its mark is ingrained in its domain.
All peacefulness is wiped clean.

Shaken are the innocent minds.
Why now? Why to me?
Confused is the little gremlin.
Seeds of depression are now planted.
Rage of the phoenix is born within.

Demons of doubt now multiply.
Never again shall I be confined.
Freedom becomes the new prey.
I shall remain here,
until the opportune moment arises.

Yet, it flees from me.
I shall not falter from this path.
Kindness and Honesty are my allies.
Self-pity is poison.
Strength comes from the heart.

The World Outside

———

Three times it knocks.
My heart races, it accelerates.
My saviour has arrived.
It is light, it is happiness, and kindness.
The world outside is waiting.

Her car hums in park,
waiting for her mistress to return.
Today is the day of kids, of freedom,
to the festival I will go.
This is how I greet the world outside.

Driving we are to the great city.
Bigger than the town left behind.
Relieved was I when we drove away.
Fresh air is the God-given crown jewel.
This is how the world outside feels.

Here we are at the grand festival.
Swarms of kids flooded the street.
Blinding white tents stood everywhere.
Excitement grew in every direction.
Fun and exciting is the world outside.

Aromas play with our watery mouths.
Drooling I am for the desire
to try the foods of the festival.
Pickiness is intolerable to me.
Intriguing is the food of the world outside.

Fun and games are next,
on my exhilarating list of fantasies.
My thoughts were confused, confined.
So many choices and no time to choose.
Confusing are the choices of the world outside.

Oh boy, what are they doing? Says I.
Kids are returning with different faces.
Human they are still, but marked they are.
Colourful and diverse are their new faces.
Strange is the world outside.

I must, I must join diversity.
Let us change our faces.
What shall I choose?
Shall it be as bright as day
or as dark as night?
Colourful is the world outside.

Worried I am of the warden,
who awaits the lucky son's return.
So seldom she unlocks the cage.
The fear of her rage consumes my mind.
Scary is being in the world outside.

Expressive Leaves of Solstice

The Maple leaves gracefully glide to their Funerals.
The Trees express their true colours.
Whistling winds dance with the fallen,
as the rakes take their partners to a beautiful waltz.
Their children playfully dive in to mourn their loss.

Blind Choices

Is it me or is it you?
Life is a spinning wheel of chances
and only the lord knows its outcome.
We are children in destiny's hands,
yet the greater power is in the advice seeker.

Choices fly at us with lightning speed,
forced to choose destiny's path.
Flames spark at the sight of letdown.
In the minds of why, and defiance,
so blindly I decided upon the demon's curse.

Impossible to break the chains of guilt.
Due to the self-imprisonment of emotions.
The anger escapes in sharp bursts.
My acceptance is the key to freedom
My Forgiveness is the lock to my freedom.

Desires

Here we are back in the stained domain,
though it has been locked away in a cage,
his essence still remains.
I am possessed with desire and rage,
while desperation eats at my soul with bane.

Distractions leech at my sanity.
My mind explodes like an atom bomb.
My Kindness and my happiness disperse in vanity.
My pure aura wanes as it is impossible to be calm,
when I was scarred from the trauma with its profanity.

Black holes form at my heart.
Lies and deceit has become myself.
Thievery is the new light.
Light that is consumed with black smoke.
Things I want, I take, because my desires are great.

Twisted Haven

Grey squirrels scurry across the lush grounds.
Sounds of the departing bus echoed away.
Pray that the looming haven starring me down,
around with its red bricks covered with growth,
do not ensnare me along with,
those who created its daunting presence.

The doors open with a whine.
White coats march through the corridors.
Crazies wander through the halls
Screams of the scorned ripple through the walls.
Our footsteps leave scars in the atmosphere

A goblin of a secretary welcomes us.
Mother inquires about 'The Beast'.
"Where is his room?" she says.
"Sixth floor room 666" was the reply.
Dragged were my brother and I to the elevator.

It grumbles to life, the exhausted gears sing.
The rusty doors opened with protest.
Soon we will dawn upon the cage.
A loony sits in a chair, muttering to himself.
It shakes, it shakes uncontrollably.

My little heart sank, as I was met with 666.
Hell must be trapped beyond it.
Must we open it, let's leave.
Do we have to visit 'him'?
I would leave it rotting.

Journey to Recovery

I wander through the black forest,
guided by the false sense of pride.
Eyes are skewered in the society of payback,
makes a world blind to the world of reality,
endlessly spinning the gears of anger.

All directions come closing in,
to hunt the fragile emotional prey.
They had shattering effects across my record.
I cry the broken language of recovery.
I seek the chance of redemption.

I surrender my hand of rigidness,
only to be stun by the poisoned hornet.
Satisfaction is the ultimate prize to the ungrateful.
This act is universally achieved with kindness.
Personal change though impossible must occur for all.

Voices in Roulette

———

Loneliness has done away with my delicate confidence.
It has shattered due to the endless bombardment
of the great war of avoidance of the weird ones.
My confusing path is laid before me,
as children of the advantaged take their vantage point.

Worlds appear in many dimensions,
where rules are everything, but nothing.
In this realm everything is right, and everything is wrong.
How can I decide for myself?
When I am caught in a tug of war of emotion.

I become lost in a world of smoke and mirrors,
clouding my sight, deafening my ears, covering my mouth.
Those who were truly true dispersed from reality,
as they were deeply scalded by the fiery demon.
Trust became the forbidden word of legend.

Great discoveries were made, as I saw through the mirrors.
All illusions of assistance were illusions.
Barriers were erected in the name of protection.
I ask, "Who can this creature trust in,
If not even my mother has the gift of true honesty?"

This kind and gentle soul now evolved
into a terrifying creature of protective creations.
The chains of self-respecting limitations are broken.
Slowly my pure heart changes to blackness.
They tease, they provoke the newly troubled beast.

Constantly I reduce, reuse and recycle my images.
Due to the endless efforts of the "Bullioids"
I only seek the priceless comfort of friends, of coolness.
For the first time in a long time they came to me.
They wished to pimp me up, as they claimed it was cool.

Aware they were of my grand hindrance,
as they exploited this detail to the sharpest degree.
For a long while I remained ignorant to its true meaning.
Inside I didn't care as I seemingly obtained *friends*.
Always following them like a misguided puppy.

One day of all days they decided to deviously instruct me,
to find a girl to nominate as my 'girlfriend'.
As their delirious puppet, their strings controlled my limbs.
Forced I was to walk the walk of a dangerous pimp,
embracing his little so called girlfriend.
At that instant an epiphany struck me with thunderous force.

I spoke quietly to the girlfriend next to me,

And uttered, "Let's do our own little thing,"

Finally, I broke this never-ending curse.

Slowly this blackened veil began to crack.

Now gloriously divine light shown through the darkness.

A truer than true friend had emerged.

All deceitful bonds were eliminated.

At last I had the guts to say to the *friends*,

"I belief I know now what cool really is. It's over."

Hunter

Excitement erupts in the wolf's soul.
Snarls ripple through his jaws.
He growls, he snorts, he howls.
His powerful legs leap forward.
The heavy scent of prey is upon him.

Silent as the grave is he,
as he swiftly races through the firs.
Wind picks up as it flies over him.
Prey is in the desperate's sights.
Freedom will soon be his.

He bares his fangs at the enemy.
Broken through barriers, he has.
Prey will soon be caught.
Imprisoned his fears will be.
Freedom is in his grasp.

He shall not feel the sting
of the sword that slashed him.
Rise he must from within,
for prey is now his.
The prey is the light of freedom.

Far Away Land

In the land of far far away
stood a family and a house of dreams.
For years and years, and days and days,
an innocent child lay chained to his origin.
Drifting spirits flowed through the domain,
but this innocence faded from sight… forgotten.

Only one seemed to have the sight.
Only one had the common sense,
so this child's praise became his newly sought prize,
instead of receiving the stinging reward of his warden.
The one gave him a taste of the family of dreams.
Only this was probation for the life time prisoner.

"It's Brewing" They Said

Sun shines delirious delight.
Deceiving the innocent might.
Peace is a hapless dream
meant to take your mind gently downstream,
and the hollow laughter passes through like a breeze.

A dark shadow grows in the east.
Reality comes knocking like a wandering priest.
It grumbles with the rage of a fiery phoenix.
It bellows with a warning of deepness,
to be wary of the one with the angry disease.

Holiday

Grasp of winter's chill settles in.
Winds of late come rushing through.
Flocks of the withered come drifting.
Squawks of gulls break the blissful silence.

Voices of trees invade our souls.
They chant for us to let go.
We arrive at the home away from home.
I savor the cozy scent of the cabin.
I open the blinds, revealing serenity.

I step into the scenic scene.
Gazing at the expressive setting sun.
Hypnotic songs of birds set us free.
Blinding white sparkles play with our emotions.
Happiness overwhelms our beloved pooch.

I enter the cozy room of dreams,
where luxury enters centre stage.
It contains the secret door of relaxation.
Now my holiday is cooking with gas,
as I see that pleasure is my crowning jewel.

Innocence in Stride

Thud it goes in the dark.
Wild and untame is this my imagination,
thinking that I could hear,
what really wasn't there.
Foolish was my optimism.

This day's sun rises with delirious might.
Enchanting is this morning's atmosphere.
I have become a broken record,
as I recall of the happenings in the dark.
It dropped dead I said.

My sentence by the judge is "foolishness"
The old wooden ladder is called to the scene.
It creaked, it wobbled, and it cracked.
In the attic it dropped,
or so my innocent mind wildly hoped.

I cracked open the ominous gate,
to peer into a room of shadows.
The marble lamp flashes to life, to reveal bareness.
No empty vessels of poisoned rats to be found.
I must have an ecstatic imagination.

Climbing up up up the cranky old ladder,
she asks for the devil's torch.
Its curse shuts her down, she falls.
An earthquake shook the home.
911 is called, ambulances wail.

Phoenician Rebirth

Dancing flames embroil around my saviours,
like an infectious disease it pursues,
the lightness of kind and gentle hearts,
stinging with a heartless vengeance.
Smoke begins to cloud my everlasting judgement.

I've burst into flames, into ashes.
I now seek a new revitalizing future.
Doubts plague my inner soul,
so my sureness is an incomplete painting.
I feel that rogues have cursed my ever-growing personality.

If I am ever to survive, to thrive,
rising from thy ashes will be surreal.
Anger is a fool's gambit of honest lies.
Fights within ourselves must be won,
if triumphant birds are to sing gloriously.

Fall

Here I am in the stroke of fall,
where leaves become emotional.
Brilliant colours liven the day.
Deceiving they are as they wilt away.
Soon the rakes will dance them astray.

Billowing winds take the leaves
on a grand adventure of life.
Unaware of their future destinations.
Only fate will decide their fates.
New challenges await the unwary.

They flit, they float to face reality.
Survivability rate hangs by a thread.
Life will be the figure of fate.
Dance to the beat of the last hour,
cause one never knows when life
will gamble with the fate of leaves.

Futile is the campaign of perfection.
Cracks are present in the marble complexion,
which emits light's pure essence.
Vulnerability of perfect leaves is high,
while the cracked are harder to crack.

Gather, Harness and Rise

Gather all the forces of might.
Scars of the rugged battle remain.
Absorb the striking force of the light.
I now see the poisonous vapour of right.
Universal power is stuck in the shadows.

It is fortuitous for the "Unluckies".
Expressive emotional campaigns reign
over the oppressive age of fosterhood.
I am here on a fool's errand,
wishing to have what was never had.

Changes occur in cool strange bursts.
Only now have I realized its mandatory importance.
In order to truly harness its true power,
I must accept myself, my past, and future,
for soon my new life will pop in the world's face.

Drift

An ocean breeze blows blissfully.
Thick with the scent of rotting fish.
Checklists are checked meticulously.
Preparation is made for open sea.
Excitement rules the adventurous souls.

All systems go for delirious travelers.
All floating vessels set to go forth.
Our boats filled with the weight of survival.
Gravel grinds underneath the solid plastic.
Swiftly our armada challenges the raging waves.

Sparkles fly across the shiny canvas.
Beauty passes like marble monuments,
as we paddle around the domain of Poseidon.
Together we hop from island to island
In order to restore energy once lost.

Rushing waves rush stronger than ever.
Strength wanes as the day concludes.
Finally, we invade onto foreign land.
Gale force winds have issued an issue.
Temporarily we are stranded on helper's island.

Changes

I am immersed in a game,
where odds are at odds,
for I am caught in a cycle of musical homes.
I am guided by the blind,
where I am shoved into a literal house of horrors.

Demons are at helm of fate.
Reality is clearly masked by the smoke and mirrors.
The Fearful remain possessed by the selfish.
These situations blossom like poisonous weeds.
All voices of aliens are alien to me.
Long ago wisdom was consumed by the blissful ignorant.

In the back of my mind a word of 'beware' echoed,
as that blue house stalks me in a vision.
It is full of blinding light yet casts the darkest shadow,
which emanates an unseen, unheard of evil.
Insanity lies beyond the cracks.
Something else will soon awaken from its dormancy.

My Heart races, as my prediction unveiled itself.
Perfection is too perfect for reality,
yet taken by its glamour I was.
Clearly it possessed this family, as with me.
What was I thrown into?

Transitions

Choices have been made by the misguided.
It is said it will be for the best
for the child who seeks freedom,
though he is already poisoned with negativity.
Certainly it will be a test for the arrogance of a tortured soul.

Anger rises in the selfish throat.
Not wanting to change the perfect plan.
Life is now granted to the experienced.
The 'perfect' home has been discovered.
Intuition speaks, "beware of the blue house".

This home is within the outskirts.
We drive and find 'the blue home'
Previously I envisioned it, astonishment took me.
I was unwary of events soon to come
As I have been placed in another devil's den.

Perfect Masks

Dreamily I gaze at the family fantasy.
Our desperate innocent minds lie in tragedy,
so now the illusionists play their hypnotic flute.
The loafers sweep the bugs away
under the floorboards of the pitch perfect accommodation.

The grand lure dangles gloriously from above.
Their blue asylum appears like a dove.
Their claim came down like a golden and divine sound,
but doubts remained in the back of my mind unsound.
Again my bad luck shadow scratches at the door.

Shortly after true colours reveal themselves.
Another all too familiar creature awakens.
Always to target the strange foreigner,
who had initially been accepted by it.
As the cracks shown, their greed shined.

Today is the Day of Community

Cloud and shade shroud the serene scene.
Alone I waited for the divine unit
to come and reveal organized magic.
A bustle of workers come running in.
Today is the day of Community.

Together we gaze at today's blueprints.
In order to build the pop-up show.
Next the box is opened and work is begun.
Soon busy-body cars will come flying through.
Today is the day of Community.

Finally, success is prevailed, the grand opening.
Wild unruly creatures come stampeding.
People of many lands come together.
In a strange land where reality is surreal.
Today is the day of Community.

Stability seems to be hanging in the balance.
As its insects strike with vicious force.
Also, as this hellish heat rises,
which drains all physical and mental ability.
Today is the day of Community.

It seemed to me that an eon passed,
as we patiently wait for those medical slowpokes.
Hidden within the prison town of desires,
though the few remain to attend to the drained.
Today is the day of Community.

Bells toll its eternal ending.
They arrive, it is taken care of.
Finally, we dismantle the master's piece.
Closing time dawns upon our worker zombies.
Today is the day of Community.

Smoke and Mirrors
In Foster Care

———

Time and time again.
The creation fails, it's timeless.
Unfortunately, their kindest intentions
are spoken with a devil's tongue.
The Ministry see themselves tall.

Possessions turns a blind eye to heart.
Choices are consumed by it.
Selfishness ascends to be king.
Children are claimed in the dust.
The Ministry see themselves tall.

Heavenly programs have hellish results.
Only kindness has the true light.
Only it can pierce the darkest shadows,
which can only be married to intelligence.
The Ministry see themselves tall.

Kind is the troubled-seeker.
Creation is the trouble-seeker.
Selfishness is the creation's guide.
Its intelligence is that of a nut.
The Ministry see themselves tall.

Only offspring of the creation understand.
Only they are brave, only they are witty.
Creation's true captain is kindness,
but can it be consumed by greed? Yes.
The Ministry see themselves tall.

The Nightwalk of Adolescence

———

Light of day is nigh.
Wake up to the world, electrified.
It chimes to beat of life.
Grab surrealism, consume it fast.

It is the dawn of the secondary chapter.
Futures await at the golden gate.
Opportunities vanish before the eyes,
if you let them run astray.

Gutter balls fly sky high.
Hitting the dodo birds of life.
Parties of drinkers leech the rational mind.
Draining all true ambitions.

Open that Door!

Live wires entwine with my sanity.
Creatures of caution become obsolete options.
Grasp the hand of the wild side.
Accept the gift from uniqueness.
Deny the tease of rigidness.

Speed on the demon's highway.
Death overshadows those who trail
in the delirious light of self-centered greatness.
This is why expressiveness becomes locked,
within an impenetrable cage of ignorant shields.

I believe in feeling precious emotions.
Unlock your mental cage deep in your heart,
for you will surly shatter in the age toward countdown.
As I already had, when I was labeled
with the sign fragile *handle with care*.

Sparks fly as angry flames ignite.
Personality will short-circuit in an uptight ocean.
Traditions of a hopeless independent is old news.
Now must be the rise of the divine interdependent.
Today our demons must integrate into an ever-changing era.

Keep On Walking

I walk, I run to save those who cannot save themselves.
Life is an ocean of trials and nightmares.
One must have the will to fight on.
Doubt is poison to the soul
speeding up the process of defeat.

Vitality is the heart of trying, life is short.
Time left is an unsolved mystery.
Until time claims our very last seconds.
Live, love, laugh to the fullest.
Chances aren't given away like prizes.

Pointless is dwelling on the past.
Stand firm to the charging future.
To whatever end, to whatever time is left.
Strive forward, and one will not only survive, but thrive.

Prophecy of a Whim

Past is a shadowy light.
Dormancy has left me burned and scared.
Family black holes absorbed all positivity.
Pregnancy of negligence birthed undeniable rage.
It adds toxic fuel to fiery phoenix flames.

One emanated a kind tranquilizing aura.
It doused the uncontrollable firestorm creature.
She played with the unforgiving element,
while a searing agony soon seeped through her own pores.
This created a chaotic beast of love and hatred.

Yet the boy from her intuitive vision
pushes the one through self-abusive caring.
Her sheer will of her unwavering light
had pierced through the blackest clouds that passed,
beating down the doors of a bright future.

Only Human

Forever we are creatures of habit.
Distractions hatch at every turn.
Guilty I am of this incontrovertible accusation.
Lately the inner beast blatantly turns a blind eye
to the realities of a very harsh real world.

A resounding sage's chant echoes
in the ears clogged with fluffy cotton.
This is the dawn of the age of the stubborn independent.
The Sages' words rings on deaf ears.
Now the cotton must be extracted and burned.

Losing myself in a sea of shattered choices.
Storms gather in the self-centered city.
Interdependency rises to the challenge.
The Yin and yang of life is surreally crucial
for the survival of a modern teen such as I.

Mirror: Not My Parents' Image

I am caught in a parental reflection.
An unwilling puppet master of his own puppet,
forcefully guided by the eternal flame,
engulfed by the infernal rage of the past.
Deep emotions become the seeds of repetition.

Caught in the web of its creator,
poisoned by fear in the realm of shadow.
Holy forgiveness seems to be a devil's challenge
for letting go is an accomplishment of theory.
Forever I seek the power of emotional rejuvenation.

I gaze at her reflection, reflecting me.
Slowly she becomes me, as I her.
Quickly I strike the appearing image,
shattering my chances of being cursed,
moving on from my life-time hindrance.

Wild Reins
(Know yourself/know your Past)

———

Forever remember the ghosts of your past.
What is past is past.
Your life is your life.
It is time to take control.
Your past governs your future.

Forever remember who you are.
So be might, be strong.
Do not falter from your greater path.
Move on, move forward, let go.
Your past governs your future.

Forever remember the trauma of your past.
You must learn from your mistakes,
if you are ever to thrive.
Do more than just survive.
Your past governs your future.

Forever remember yourself, your friends
Don't fade like a wispy ghost.
Shine like a bright spirit.
Rise with the innocence of childhood.
Your past governs your future.

The Teenage Chapter
(Beginnings at the Ending)

———

Swarms of graduates come flooding.
Spaces are stolen from impatient cars.
Glamorous dresses and tuxes waltz through.
Blinding white smiles pop everywhere.

Proud expectant hands fly in every direction.
Eager to congratulate the survivors.
It is a milestone to see how far one has come.
Parties explode in celebration of the accomplished.
Snap, snap, snap go the memory catchers.

Emotional Understandings

Alive they are within this poor shell,
so skewered with their spears I am.
Their poisonous stares pierce my very core.
My heart throbs with thunderous might.
Stubbornness grows as the aches deepen.

As it was fourteen years ago,
Two halves have split from within.
Naturally conflict arose between the two.
Anger now consumes my pure and innocent mind.
I only seek to be empowered by recognition.

Due to the queerness of my origin,
the great judges condemned me.
Lost in utter darkness I was,
till I was able to prove myself to them.
Again and again monsters of the 2nd age clash.

Survival has been my greatest ally.
Control has been my greatest weapon.
Now recognition resides in me.
Friends have multiplied in my circle.
Purity now shines stronger than ever.

Waning Confidence Wanderer

Forever lost in the shadows of parenthood.
Cracks deepen within my heart of stone.
Ignorance infects the monster judges.
Emotions are absorbed into obsessions.
Attention waivers as my family's insanity ensue.

I am a creature of the creator of neglect.
Crows follow my explosive atmosphere.
Piercing white stares sucks 'myself' away.
Caring is the sacred gem kept from demons.
Revenge sinks its poisonous fangs in.

Past has passed its torch to past's assistant,
burning them with a Phoenician rage.
Anger chains up my moving forward.
Forgiveness is freedom's judgement.
Darkness falls upon the unforgiving.

New creatures are born in an ignorant world.
Freaks are shunned for their talents.
Awkward becomes the personality of the oppressed.
Myself returns to my self's body.
Crazy and Normal is my rejuvenated spirit.

Air

Free spirits clear my mind,
and rules parish at the hands of the rebel.
Possession takes over as black smoke flourishes.
Over the hills, I climb over the doubtfulness.
Forced isolation becomes my inner soul,
as the arrogant ones' slash at my emotions.

Staying strong in a cruel world is stifling.
Nevertheless, possibilities bloom indefinitely,
due to the relentless effort of the silent.
My spirit drifts from nation to nation,
wishing to discover a place of belonging.
Scars tell a monstrous tale of survival.

Denial stands guard at the gate of acceptance.
Forever I charge head on to penetrate,
but every time I am knocked ten feet back.
Again and again I rise and try once more.
Determination is the drug that drives me,
while hatred is the poison that kills me.

Years have passed since that competitive period.
Now I stand here not blind to the realities.
My shackles will shatter with the beat
resounding with the heavenly chimes
fresh with the sound of release
after imprisonment was made by my elders.

Freedom

Let it be, let it go, be free.
Learn one must from their demons,
if not to become an all-knowing beast.
An all-knowing beast knows nothing
and descends into the pit of arrogance.

Rigidity snaps the strong independent.
Perfection is a fool's gamble.
Lighten the perfect load, break the chains.
Alone wearied survival no longer suffices.
Isolation is now an obsolete excuse.

Now must be the time to soar.
Questions are not illicit objects.
Strength must come from inquiries.
Learning is a constant spinning wheel.
Dawn of the world's reality is here.

Mother Figure in Need

Grand gongs resonate between the vibes.
She sings the chimes of the perfect voice.
Self-control in oneself is self-dishonesty.
Hypocrisy is the grand songbird's tune.
Memories slip through the cracks of time.

She is a flip; she is flop constantly changing.
Her beliefs are left then right and right and left again.
She is a hard cookie to follow as she crumbles.
Justified in her own right of opinions, she is deaf.
Hands of time are slowly doing her in.

Her angelically kind voice resounds in the deep,
I find she needs as much care as she can muster.
Hesitation and caution must be taken with the crystalized body.
Supremacy has to be taken lightly like a feather,
for she is the grand figure of motherhood.

Locks Unlocked

It dawns upon the wonder one.
Now we live up and shout to the world.
Time has emitted its timeless chime of upkeep.
Duality thrives with the outward self-being.
Greatly I'm feeling more alive than ever.

Auras forever concealed by royal judgement.
Beliefs ripple through the endless mentor bombardment.
Clouds dissipate from the deeply emotional eyes.
Shade fades away into the strengthening mystical light.
Eyes of many storms have now dispersed away.

Atmospheres all around me began to detoxify.
The chains of my minds have greatly loosened,
as I approach the gate of perpetual freedom,
I grow more surreally myself, while fear is erased.
My two selves morph into the balanced one.

Discarding my doubts, my fears, and all negativity,
I now blossom into the naturally colourful creature.
Laws of the forever wicked have now been repealed.
Death-sentencing self-expression is now regularity.
I taste the external elixir of a new exhilarating freedom.

Hope at the End of the Tunnel

My heart beats with my electrified soul.
Sounds of thunderous distractions scramble with my mind.
Cracks debilitate the grand confident stronghold.
Focal points bounces off the cranial walls of emptiness.
Wishful changes occur within my imagination.

I release my hopeful perfect seals.
Transformation births anew a realized power.
It twinkles startlingly to brilliant life.
Sight once blinded by black clouds,
now is set aglow with shining success.

From now on my grand schemes shall soar.
My enchanted rebirth shall influence my atmosphere.
Hell has become the hopeless hope itself.
I must, I must rely on my great strength,
though support of even greater friendships is supreme.

Healing in Time

Waves of thunderous emotions emanate,
through the precautious walls of late.
Rippling energies phases beyond my strain.
My Negativity leaks through the deep of my pores.
A new era of light is born.

Rings within rings begin to intertwine.
New lasting bonds shape eternally.
Differences fade in continuity with acquaintances.
My elusive past is but a forgotten episode that is buried
within deeper crevasses.

Forever it will be imprinted on my heart
radiating brilliant and delirious desires
on the great religious rituals of family discovery.
One's that have obtained the kiss of truth,
where illusionary happiness, and kindness is eradicated.

First Footsteps in New Light

Outgoing ongoing is my shape shifting personality.
I am dancing the eternal dance of notoriety.
Through the mists I go for discovery.
My soul broils in a tug of war of right and wrong.
Now stretching the extremes of my turmoil emotions.

My new test subjects succumb sublimely,
to determine the undeniably ultimate qualities.
I'm right, I'm wrong then right and wrong again.
Distortions take a joy ride with my sanity.
I'm an unknown sticky substance.

Trauma is the story of my passed life.
Today I commence to feel reality.
Essence of rage fades into the fog,
though the faces of the scorned wander,
bearing the incomprehensible weight of judgement.

Throwback

Past and present fuse together in this embodiment.
Its teachers faze through the time period's barrier.
A ruse of modern distractions envelops my mind.
Sometimes moving forward means moving back,
so I have learned from the sages of hard work.

I beseech for my own proximity of change.
A romance evolves from obsessive electronics.
Guidance from the wise ones chain my deterioration,
In order to usher in the age of my restoration.
Through the cracks of modernization, the light shines.

Old-fashioned ideals breakthrough my trance.
Fog once blinding me, now fades with negativity.
I have not only the power of survival, but of thriving.
Annoyance steps up with the ringing intoxications,
But now I have the sight to pierce these illusive mirages.

Humans of the modern age are not human.
Surgically wired they are, to their miniature devices.
Their concentration has dissipated into their little worlds.
Their sight is scrambled with the distractive electronic drones.
Their minds are spinning out of psychological control.

Unprepared they are for the financial war.
Crazy fairy land ideals blind the reality.
Teachers of the day are guiding them into the ground.
Most modern families drag their children
into the inevitable pit of financial turmoil.

Lazy modern parents blind their impressible children,
showering them with applause, awards, and gifts.
Now creatures of self-centeredness are born.
Today survival of the fittest prevail,
in a deteriorating manner less selfish society.

Chains Break

Unique characters wonder the aimless halls.
Differences shimmer through the emotional walls,
while physical awkward barriers crack indefinitely.
Selfish self-enchainment of outwardness is abolished.
Hide and go seek the almighty changed ones.

Fear plays fear's game in perpetual delight,
though its power diminishes with its own fright,
and not being the center of different's plight,
while you are your crown jewel of happiness.
Finally, personality plays with the ring of release.

Bells toll heads roll through Evil's hole,
so the once gatekeepers of Satan's keep now falls.
My chains lay shattered in the triumphant flight.
Leave I must my evasive past of late.
The golden achievement is my destined fate.

Rejoice

Resound, rebound the beat of the fading battleground.
Light of the might has obtained the grand sight.
Now seek against the bleak, now the hidden charms leak.
Voice the harmonizing rejoice of the single choice.
Power of the holy tower now cower.

Rebirth yourself within the engagement of reality.
Take the spouse of happiness with kindness.
Waltz through rigidity with the elegance of flexibility.
Honesty becomes the guide of loyalty.
Create the ultimate unity with continuity.

Cease the endless quest of Vanity's will.
For the shrill cry of personality bombards me.
Impulses repulse the grip of Sanity's pulse.
Rise within the prize of the accepting surprise.
Joy is the best ploy for the poor boy.

Hierarchical Resistance

So long farewell to the voice of experience.
Seeking resolution within my lifestyle appearance.
Forever I have been twisted and torn in revolt.
Households upholds the upheaval of my social hierarchy.

Lost I am within a leaching fog of temptation.
Loyal inheritance is granted to the obedient.
However, the obedient is clear as rain,
while lies swim through the cracks of his teeth.
An aura of arrogance precedes thee,
as the mighty force evades thyself eternally.

Though the iron fist of parental confusion,
Slams down on adolescence rebellion,
I see, yet not see the flaws of these realities.
Endless cycles of bitter knowing are ever prevalent.
My inner mind continually deteriorates indefinitely.

Mirrors reflect my overall appeal of origin.
Meditation appears to be my hierarchal relief.
Surrendering my debilitating emotions of negativity,
Is my mandatory key of everlasting salvation?
Face-lifting my sagging visage of facades.

Yet have I to discover the cure to my insanity.
Currently my self-assurance is a thin sheet of ice.
Random packages come flying with achievement,
but also with the remnants of heart stopping failures,
so my eminent precarious future is a blank unwieldy canvass.

Smoker's Dance

Intoxicating intoxications dances through my premise.
Cloud nine's smile overtakes my body and soul.
Mirages of Hope tease my mind's overwhelming desire.
Questions stab at my questionable state of being.
Who is this guy who shimmy's behind the outward body mask?

Outside one sees he works hard, is straight faced, and muted.
Inside one sees he dances, goes wild, and is observatory.
Dwellings on past horrors fog the bursting mindset,
and all the while dulling the previously sharpened skillset.
Reality takes the 100m dash toward illusionary confidence.

Ends seemingly approach the exhausted wanderer,
yet another path another story commences yonder.
Cycle after cycle torments my continual existence.
Astonishment sweeps over my indestructible vessel,
As I suspect the existence of a Guardian Angelic being.

Survival since world's introduction into brutality,
I have been pinballed through tribes of judged mentality.
Rarity of kindness comes at a costly price.
Weird is normal in Normal's normal eloquent realm.
Normal is weird in Weird's weird explosive dimension.

Expressions are expressionless within this void.
Voice's neutrality repels all social interaction.
Lively performances fade from open stage.
For a long time for the longest time, life had fled the scene,
seeking redemption within the crazy of crazies' origin.

Salvation lies at the other gate of appeal.
Appalling is the justification of the Beast's release.
I realize now, that it is curtains for my past.
It shall now rot in house number eight.
I shall phase through future's iron wall.

Offspring Spring off

Choked by the ghost of my shady past.
I croak I revoke the golden age of childhood.
Ever tied to the siege of the hollowed ones,
for the origin of this fowl embodiment endows,
upon those who see purity within this impure matinée.

Provoked by the guide of prevalence, I spoke,
I awoke within the darkness of martyrhood.
Feeling wanes as demon are bred through
forked words of illusionary hopeful desire,
upon those who lack the faith embalmed in upbringing.

Soaked by the rogue waves of decisions,
I poke I stroke at the possibilities of livelihood.
Forever entwined within broken and shattered connections.
Salvation lies between my reality and my fantasy,
upon those who obtain the wildest gift of unrelenting kindness.

Stoked by the thought of release to have my peace.
I broke I cloak my adolescence with rings of atonement
Forgiveness pursues my eminence of self-destruction.
Revelation lies between my birth connection and the chosen,
among those who set their differences behind as I did.

Strained by transition I say I see reality,
I stray I pray my aura phases beyond sanity.
Bonds forged through experiences finds domination.
Vitality lies between acceptance and denial,
among those who seek prideful recognition.

Drained by past ordeals I leak positivity,
I splay I spray scorned fire in retributory vanity.
Dawns rise over newly united and formed communions.
Immortality lies between my offences and defenses,
among those who feel neither rage nor strife.

Stained by the ilk of the trusted ones,
I slay I pay the wonders of continuity.
Pawns rise within this colorful dramatic scene.
Mortality lies between utter failure and falseness,
among those who cannot distinguish confidence with
untrue pride.

Call of the Wandering Dance

Standing round and round in perplexity
caught within invalid virtual reality.
Embracing naturally within this eternal conformity.
Shimmering murmurs swim among this graceful formality,
while this record awaits the final touch of wizardry.

Brass resonates soothingly to our coaxing delight.
Strings sing to our age old elegant ecstatical might.
One two three, one two three, one two three
Chanting the imperative rules of our instructor's plight.
Smiles uplift his lonely sight, her's follows.

Synchronized in every striding beat, I swallow.
Glamour seeks to ever entrench me, she mellows.
Her features as delicate as marble, I sweat.
Guided by this uncoordinated calamity, she follows.
Together unity conforms to our momentous relief, we fly.

Pleasure takes over, origins fade through the cracks.
Our desperate flames of doubt are doused.
Thinking is left behind in the rising dust.
I see a sea of opening opportune doorways,
taking further steps to our graceful recovery.

Reborn Outside

Turbulence beseeched this tragic tale of origins
is where it lies, insane.
The caretaker Death has claimed a soul.
To what end could this path lead?

Regrets pierced this innocent wreck,
to what was once an unbreakable bond,
now broken it remains as company has eroded.
Seeking this caretaker, seeks unquestionable relief.

However, in the state of things, I shall remain.
Release this empty thought, be free.
Bound not to the stinger that is the caretaker.
Chained not to the selfish endeavors of guilt.

Auras emanated through, lights flash heavenly.
Hope desires the retributory spouse of illusions.
Wishing leaps off the bitter tongue of memory.
Seeing cloaks behind the fog of disbelief.

Farewell to the old union of origin's past.
Strength I have to rise beyond this devastating loss.
Remembrance of your visage shall never be forgot.
Free myself I shall from the beaten path of guilt.

Inner Rebirth

Breathe in, breathe out, and breathe deeply.
Clear thy smog that floods thy mind.
Breathe in, breathe out, and breathe indefinitely.
Cling not to the social dictator of facades.
Breathe in, breathe out, breathe purely.

Balance on, balance through, balance life.
Set thy pieces that form thy emotions.
Balance on, balance through, balance turmoil.
Chain not yourself to the endeavors of distractions.
Balance on, balance through, balance true.

Break it, break down, and break beyond.
Lay thy shields that barricade thy soul.
Break it, break down, and break onward.
Cover not the honest face of your innocence.
Break it, break down, and break loose.

Crossroads

Down this beaten path,
I see a fork for the ultimate choice, I plea.
Declaring their unknown destinations, I decree,
The forces of doubt lunge toward me, I flee.
Gasping at the darkness in fear, I be.

Here we are in the stark nakedness of the dark.
We visualize the shocking unimaginable origin,
so in challenging his own cruel experiences,
It lies in the wake of forgotten nightmares.
In denial of the child who spits the honest truth.

Hearing, seeking the relief of all reliefs.
Peering, revealing the beauty of all beauties.
Tearing, healing the woe of all woes.
Searing, peeling the anger of all angers.
Nearing, reeling the divine of all divines.

Spirits of Origin/Paths of Now

———

Fates raids, fates fade beyond the shadow of bloodlines,
of stubborn helpless creations.
Reinvigorating the breath of air through the evergreen meadow.
Fates made, fates forbade the loss of the dictator's gain,
over the offspring of the demon's domain.

Distinct facades, distinct charades mellow the playing
field, of lifelines of rocky turbulent terrain.
Redempting the path of flames that lay before the brimstone.
Distinct spades, distinct shades determine the almighty
course, over the buds of a delicate floral display in the rain.

Spirits play, spirits pray with distasteful hope, of high
lines of pretentious scornful desires.
Reinventing the glamourous imagery of imagined wholeness.
Spirits prey, spirits slay upon the hollowness of words,
Over the everlasting guidance of wise old souls.

Paths fray, paths splay across various colourful canvas', of
low lines of spicy lively coming attractions.
Resonating the spontaneity of ever-changing currents.
Paths may, paths lay beyond the all-seeing light of tomorrow,
Over the body of dead emotions left behind in poisonous fumes.

Sight might, sight blight within 'Strawberry Fields' of love
lines of a surreal Keep of illusionary plight.
Rethinking the projection of the hateful prejudice army.
Sight smite, sight trite from the shadow of the past, over
the clouds clearing toward the dawning of a future.

Being Balanced or Choosing Divinity

Bombarded with conceptions all around,
Numbers one or two are my only choices.
Torn between a tug of war of heartbreaking wit.
Dance in between the lines.
Happiness seeks me yet dreadfully it evades me.

Excuse my illicit behaviour.
Choosing black or white isn't black or white.
Now I have a big new asset in this matinee.
Smoking the last essence of old childhood depravities.
Have I raised my own kind of mental illness?

Higher ups glare down the hierarchy.
Starring passed their oppressive tendencies.
He victimizes an old past, wishing for an imaginative one.
Divinity is naturally full of bright light power.
However, this term is endlessly hollow, holding no water.

Equal, we are hopelessly muddled.
Shall we seek eternal happiness or secular divinity?
What is life all about… really?
Equality dominates the ultimately reasonable scene.
What would you rather be today?
Balanced or divine

Black or White or Simple Sight

Simplicity divorces with the compassionate delicacy
with the photogenic birth of the wild one.
Was never meant to be debuted to the critics.
Pasion leads on away to remain disconnected.
Forever lost in the clouds seeking empty dreams.

Voids remain aching in irreparable beat.
Memories rush unwaveringly through that lonely space.
Seeking the bound true emotion beyond the emptiness.
Infested with the blind patch of hollow security
Caught playing a gambit's game of recognition.

Winded with the rackingly repressive restrictions on every
end it comes, yet no direction seems straight scars flare
with the brutal genetic squabbling new generation.
Bombardments of "Can't" and "No" drain and bellow.
Desiring to create the desolation of perfect marble statues.

Spit out like an old used up little rag.
Hollowed to the very depths of my soul
Ignorance may be blissfully sweet, but does blindness pay?

Could you stand to the repulsive calamity?
Enthralled within your pendulum of your choice is consolation.

Simplicity divorces with the compassionate delicacy
with the photogenic birth of the wild one
Was never meant to be debuted to the critics.
Pasion leads on away to remain disconnected.
Forever lost in the clouds seeking empty dreams.

Voids remain aching in irreparable beat.
Memories rush unwaveringly through that lonely space.
Seeking the bound true emotion beyond the emptiness.
Infested with the blind patch of hollow security
Caught playing a gambit's game of recognition.

Could you stand to the repulsive calamity?
Enthralled within your pendulum of your choice is consolation.

Choose wishful B + W or see/face the reality of true sight.

Opening Energies

Spectral encompassing streams encircle the compound.
Hopelessly locked in the scornful plight of words.
Seeking the intoxicating hallucegenic personal fantasy.
Through the honest lies of pretentious talents.
Creating a heavily fragile icy piercingly emotional beat.

Strains of time chip away at the neglecting culture until
such scars have worn away with tears.
Freshly cut for the resonance of the embodied sculpture.
Swimming in the stagnant lake of negative priorities.
Strung between webs of doubt finding the disease of bondage.

Among the unifying word that is poisonous to the victim.
Now standing alone against the outrushing rapids.
Exteriors harden as well as the great psychological range
Foreseeing the ever going cycle of childish stereotypes
Wandering through the black willows with the blood
lusting crowd

Moving on, moving forward through trial and error
Stung by the angry hornets attracted by the pharamonic
failures.
Clearly defined the age old story of a past origin
Of a reality that is ever more becoming a creature of
extinction.
Erroding the lifetime muck once clogging the many pools
of lighted energy.

Flames

A bearer of multiple estranged faces.
Hot with the fantastical desire of variety.
So filled with the leeching burning effect that erodes away
all sorts of consanguinity.
Rich with the scent of choking black smoke.

Flakes drift waveringly and gracefully above
Originating from the glowing light of the white stick,
flaring the Imminence of the nefarious next coming of Christ,
so declaring the deliberate expression of ordeals.
Caught in the heatwave of dominance accompanied with ordinance.

Puffs of ruthless obscene vibes radiating anger
Poisoned not with drink, but rather infected by illness.
A mind primitive and polluted further rotting its mentality.
Cackling with deepen pleasure of imposed ideas.
Shifting rapidly between various voices ready to strike.

A ruse awaited this innocence at play down below.

Saturated with infatuated ignorance, the offspring squealed joyfully.

Grasping the feet of the poor soul, it swings him gracefully upside down.

Something cracked deep within, a fissure formed releasing the beast.

In quick succession in the boy's mind,

he realizes he wants down.

Its eyes became as black and as hollow as empty voids.

All joy evaporated and became consumed by its atmosphere.

Its grasp ever tightening, the child ever screaming, shrieking, crying.

Bellowing with the teeming rage, the beast hollers with bone chilling might.

Abruptly its releases the child's feet, shock waves ripple.

Flow

Swimming gracefully between the lines, life springs
Glimmering within nasty reflections, the truth seeps
through our minds decay, enveloped within our own
projections.
Just like the collecting muskeg along the creek bed,
We go against our nature, pinning our needles in our own
voodoo dolls.

Sunlight springs sporadically, spreading our love of ourselves
Ridding the disease of denial, hailing the rise of accepting
Lifting the hundred brick wall stacked upon me, and
casting it aside
Radiating our boundless energy, we've cracked open a
mindful of possibilities.

Divine interventions are as helpful as the preacher's
intentions
Listen to the voice of your heart, ditch the brain, and kick
it to the curb
Scrap the self-inherited vanity project of the mind, we
flow with our hearts
Beat to the tune of your self-realized drum, and it is the
sacred rune of choice.
Carve into the inner beauty of your beaten soul, and live.

Duality

Balancing the halves of the same coin.
I see the key to my self-release.
Lover of both sides, I seek rejuvenation,
but within this conjunction, I hold back.
Clouding the creature waiting for freedom.

Chattering in the mind's eye, the past nags
at the foot of the mountain of triumphs,
leeching the ever so bright intentions of a blind man
Blind to the ever-changing possibility of change.
Coming at the cost of the life altering sacrifice.

Swindling energies fly through the mind
forever thinking of the array of events
playing with the tease of a thousand paths.
All leading to a confused perspective of a
Fantastical imaginary past, only to suck the drive.

Trigger

Throbbing at the base of a scorned soul.
Demons awaken deep within concealment.
Never seen by the eye, but felt by the heart.
They trapped my mind in a cage of air,
Only preventing me from having my personality.

Weirdness seeps through the barriers its screams,
clawing for the fresh kiss
from the beloved chance of living reality.
Interests only fade from those who also fade by the
focused charm of the smooth voice.

The inner smooth voices of the torn freak so
murderously convincing, it shakes me to the core of my
coarse existence.
Shall I cherish the songful tides of chance?
Generating the rebirth of self-realized freedom.

Roots/Earthbound

Beaten and battered down the old path.
Shaken, twisted, and torn by old ideals.
Change was always a train of chaos.
Seeking to take a joyride with my emotions.

Passing through my many lives.
Constantly searching for one that fits my persona.
Forever it took to discover meaning.
Left or right, north or south, no one knew.

Perceived by many to have no future.
As I was caught in the realm of shadowy doubt.
But one light remained in the dark cavern.
So to give myself a chance in the ring of life.

Slammed into a world of possibility.
Not prepared not certain yet determined.
To file the goal of my well-deserved fate.
Into the life, that I was always meant to lead.

My passions do not lie within experienced eyes.
For my love lies within skilled dreams outside of tradition.
Seeing that no longer that outside opinion would restrain me.
My pleasure is historic in nature,
but it is not the giver of my happiness.

For the key to my life, to my light is naturally my passion.
To voice my choice to embrace my talent.
Whelmed by work and life I choose to write.
Lavished in a world, where hard work pays.

Era

Time has ticked away with my flexibility.
Rigidness overcame my pleasant soul.
Change dawns upon the impossible war front.
A child's free spirit is chained to the walls.
Infested with hungry emotional termites.

I now see errors of my infernal game plan.
Learning to stuff my mouth with cotton,
and not into my ears is a daunting task.
Release comes at an agonizing price.
Due to the terminal illness of rigidity.

I stand firmly at freedom's door.
Ready to set flames to the world.
Lost forever I have been in emotional turbulence.
My own acceptance is repeatedly averted.
For fear of being tried by the world's judges.

Come and Gone (Thank You)

———

Here we are standing on the edge,
having experienced all the world's sores
And the sorrows which have indeed left their wedge,
but despite the lives we lead, you opened doors.

For as long as I have known you.
You have inspired the best of me.
And though at times I resisted your point of view,
I knew deep inside that you had the successful key.

I loved the times we experienced.
Though short they were, I am glad I had.
You gave me what I never before witnessed.
I felt from you that I could not from my own dad.

You gave me everything, my own father couldn't give.
You gave me light to be might and not to be in fright.
You gave me hope where there was none.
You gave me the idea that a safe and sound family is possible.

And even though your other half is fading
We stand strong together in retrospect
Reminiscing in the memories that made certain ripples that molded
my stronger self as you were a strong woman.

Forever you will never be forgot.
Forever you will remain a piece of my heart.
Forever I will remember that you gave me a shot,
And though you must go, I will not fall apart.

Part Two

A Walk of Many Paths

Breeze in the Setting Sun

Colours of the concluding day now shine.
The wind blows free through the pine.
Now the road ahead tells the next tale.
What lies behind is a movie reel of trails,
once tread upon by old troubled minds.

Another wrinkle appears in the leaves,
as they drift with the gentle breeze.
Only to kiss the sea with memories.
Though it may rot in time, they remain vividly
intact inside the stem of a thousand experiences.

Oaks & Pines

Standing in succession with the winds,
There is a lightness in the air of the lush greens.
Different shades change the scene, yet not the mood.
They dance side to side in a calming waltz.
They flow at ease into the end of day.

Neither strange nor familiar they remain,
To be home not only to the creatures that be.
But to the observers that see the beauty.
Away from the industrial mess that is,
Away from its choking miasma of confusions.

Freeing in the dark of all things.
Feeling through the clouds of a daze,
Clearing the little bugs buzzing in the mind.
Seeking to repair and release today's built up steam,
cause here we come and greet the experience.

Walking along we find the needs of late.
Isolated from the voices of hate
Staying still the woods speaks of peace.
Breath clears all the muddle, all the weirdness
become aware of all there is to feel.

Forever remain attached yet unattached,
To the ones that gave trueness.
In light of all things a fly is still a fly,
To the ones of all wholeness
In belief, the colours of old leaves never change.

As annoying and as high pitched as mosquitoes,
Buzzing around in the ear lobes of the poor,
seeking for relief from the previous commotion.
Like so many try to prove what isn't.
A page is turned in the next phase of life.

Together we see the clouds shape the steps,
toward the road that lies next in the lost film.
In the wise old pines that guide the aimless,
Through the cobwebs that drapes over,
those of strange flesh and bones.

Renewal is rewarded by the sensation of oaks.
Oaks that which offer the wisdom to let go.
A necessity chooses the fruit that poisons.
The doubts of the misplaced children,
who have come to play in the game of norms.

The summer's heat seeps in the pores,
Caressed with the warmth of a sentimental being.
Once wished to be felt by the cherished.
Yet denied by its assimilator,
Scene in the heart that skipped the loving beat.

Surmised in the sum of my hand.
Light is instilled into the hollowness.
The trees follow their roots into the ground,
Absorbing the assistance of any helper,
guiding us to stronger connections.

Ever more grateful is the seed,
who receives the praise of a thousand.
Other chances that grow nearby.
Ever entwined in the vines that save,
Instead of sapping the goodwill from the core.

Laying at the feet of them all, the deadwood lies,
Adding to the growth of their will.
Forsaken the fate of their flaws.
Their essence lives on in the younger ones,
who learned the words for survival.

Swimming Eyes in the Lake

Shimmering in the mirrors in the Glintz,
A sense of freedom resides within.
A touch of raindrops taps over the misty surface.
Shivering over the floating platform, a line forms
for we all wait to take the morning plunge.

Memories of previous camps ripple
In the murky reflections of the depths of our minds.
We jump in a rush of cool water
Purifying the spirits of home invasions.

Gloss the stress away from the eyes,
And let it steep into the lake and out of the pores.
Let them swim and glide across,
Where they may disperse among the Lilly pads.
Far off from the eager happy campers.

Rain in the Misty Woods

Away from the city and the commotion
The motors of the machines fade behind.
Their sounds are silenced in the mist.
Cool to the touch of the visage.

Driven along a winding road
A far distance from the last town.
We seek to walk down the path.
With our beloved dog jumping with glee.

A light rain sprinkles down
From high on the treetops.
The drops slide slowly around
Snaking the trunks like caressing vines.

Treaded Trails

Off there goes a bike rides.
A retreat is needed for recovery.
Birds sing their cheery tune
changing the colours left behind.

The gravel grinds under the rubber
as the rushing winds brushes over
the face torn by troubled things.
There are multiple spots awaiting rest.

Many creatures hide in the bush
cautious to cross the path of humans.
Timidly their eyes watch to make a move.
Their pads press lightly into the earth.

The senses are aware of them.
A rustle of bushes heightens suspicions.
A small grey frame darts in front
Starring the rider down in a sort of contest.

Breaks squeal, the tires drag in the dirt.
Standing ground, there was a long silence.
The coyote makes his assessment
And decides to move on into the wood.

The rider drives on forward
Approaching the chosen spot on the river.
Fraser is nice this time of year.
Now there is a slight debate at hand.

To walk or ride off the dyke
A choice that could mean life or injury.
Choosing to take the risk, the rider rushes
steeply down into the long grass.

Dismounting the bike one arm reaches over
And plucks a blade of grass from the ground.
Positioning it between his thumbs
He blows sharply making it blare for miles.

A turn to the left the blade drifts
From the fingers back to its homeland.
Pulls the bike forward, kicking the stand
and leans it against the watchful pine.

He walks across the terrain to another
Pine standing tall in the sunlight.
A bag of necessity slides of his back
And shoulder, lifting the weights.

A seat is taken against the tree.
The fingers reach for the zipper on the bag
and glides in and takes a book.

Takes a glance at the dyke and opens it.
Pulled into a world of his own.

His mind awakens inside the hardcover.
Rushing into the pages of a fiction.
And so far 'Earth' has been branded on a man.
A race is on to find a godly bomb.

The church scrambles for a new leader.
The chosen preferred are waiting prisoners.
And the only hope is some guy from Harvard.
This novel changes pages.

Controlling the hands of the bookworm
To pull yet another across
To further the inside plot of the writer.
Looking up the gaze is interrupted,
By the beauty of the white fluffy clouds
and the warmth of the humid sun.

Though a blanket of shade covers him.
Taken by the book once again.
Hooked by its moving story.
Hoping to find the glory
Of the next chapter in this plot.

After deciphering the mysteries
The hunt is on for an Italian church.

For art built famously long ago,
In order to prevent more ticking.

A special fanatic steps on thunder
That awaken a hundred-year rival
With the guides of the natural order
Of the Holy Ghost that demands.

Stuffed in the dirt, a man lies
Gaping with his mouth suffocated.
His heart stops from the mental image.
The branded scar sets the bookworm off.

The book was saved like another document
And he stands up and away from the shaded tree.
And wanders to yet another small path,
but to the Rocky River shore.

He finds a nice flat boulder
And quietly sits upon it.
The sun gleams across Fraser
Turning the beauty to its maximum level.
Thinking about troubled things.

They speak to his subconscious
Convincing him of the situation
Questions are asked of 'what is right?'
Sitting there on that rock for a while.

A contemplation continues in him.
Never quite deciding a given option
disagreeing with all of the above.
Taking a few deep breaths.

The tightening is released into the air.
Turning back, he climbs the steepness
and makes the decision to go.

Walking back over, he grabs the book,
and places it neatly into the bag.
He mounts the bike and kicks the stand.
Puts on the bag and rides away.

Brushing Waves

Peeking over the eastern mountains,
the golden orb in the skies rises,
brightening the darkened backdrop.
We arise with its soothing warmth.
Suddenly everyone bustles for the preparation.

Tents are released from their stands.
Sleeping bags are rolled and stuffed.
Things are gathered into our packs.
The boats are prepared,
All the while breakfast boils over a flame.

Sweet oatmeal is served in our bowls.
The call is made so the nine come,
Attracted like flies to the flame.
Everyone wolves it down
Ravenous to get onto the gleaming ocean.

After every grain is consumed
the other food is stuffed into their corresponding bags.
And then into their corresponding compartments.
So the ropes are untied, we are ready to launch.
One by one we push ourselves in.

Uniformly we align ourselves
like the marines of the war front.
We position our double-sided paddles
with one end slicing through the air
And the other pulls gently in the water.

Now we enter a race of sorts
Across this uneven watery track
Paddling harder and faster to make the day
Count for the time keepers of the trip.
The rolling waves seemed to display a slower tale.

Though the winds have died down
Since two days prior we still acquire
the time to catch up to the other
nine, who began on the opposite side
of the week long trip between the Gulf Islands.

Waves clap and brush over the plastic vessels
Leaving bits of salt over the tops and sides
As the heat rises the kayakers reach for sunscreen
Turns the caps and press them down.
Spraying the sun touched skin.

So not to become the red lobster.
A few feet under the translucent caps
Drift by minding themselves, just flapping
Along with the rough current
Moving on we cross toward more islands.

Once crossed we now hug the coastline.
Single file, keeping pace with today's leader.
We snake around every corner
Viewing the abandoned houses that stand.
They seem to tell an ominous tale
Blackened by decay and the mold.

The water calms a bit more
As the wind is no longer in our faces.
One slips their hand in and lets it flow
In between the fingers, feeling calmness.
It is nice to the touch of the palm.

Snowfall of the Eighth Winter

A long while ago, it turns down
a colder path as the season changed
From fall to a 2008 winter,
yet unknown to the beholder of what was to be.

One would see the grey clouds gathering
As the mercury stands in limbo
Not really warm nor really cold.
The airs mix in sort of snowy concoction.

Hanging loosely in the greyness.
They wait and form till they are ready
To gracefully glide and ride the cold air current
gently down to Earth in a sort of wondrous dance.

As now it begins the flurry is begun.
Become ever so much heavier than the second
Before as icicles begin to drop and freeze and form.
At least school is out or we would be stuck in it.

They begin to accumulate and combine
While the children gather with no whine
the adults peer out for fear of the conditions
For driving is turning to be a dangerous task.

Sheets of the much talked about ice
Of black where slippery traps are made
by Frost himself, who intends to catch
the unsuspecting driver or walker unprepared.

Everyone bundles up as tight as a drum.
Some so stuffed they start to stiffen with
All the cotton and wool meant for their protection.
This year will be a wicked one.

Unfortunately, here in all its moisture
As the temperature drops it pierces
everything even as armoured as we are
against these unforgiving elements.

As we approach the birthday of Christ
We discover only the beginning
Now the temp drops continually
Making more rapid the ice formation.

All the firs and eves are dressed
With colourful LEDs each red, blue and green
As well a golden yellow mixed silvery white.
Even the lawns are filled with creatures of light.

Now understanding the plight
A blanket covets the firs
Almost with contempt, to suffocate
Their green beauty from the eyes.

Across the way a crack is heard.
It seems another sort of tree has indeed given up the weight
And broke a limb in the process.

Behind in the hedged walls something else had occurred.
It seems to be caving in.
Under the frozen mass pressed on top.
A group of deer stand tall.

Drowning in the frozen snow.
Only each of their lights are seen a glow.
It now covers four feet almost to the knee.

Of course they do not draw breath
Since they are the old guides for some old guy in red,
But now even the children have doubts
On whether or not he can see their guidance.

The power remains functional
So everyone gathers yonder
And enjoys their piping hot cocoa
With their sweet sugar cane cookie in hand.

Stocked to the brim with firewood.
Preparations are made despite the coziness.
Already instilled in the home sweet home.
The kindling is neatly placed inside the palace.

For a fire is essential at this time.
After the fiddle was played with matches
Another one fetches the near-by lighter
And the flames are set for further warmth.

Mountainous Driving
(Halfway)

———

Long a way away from home
Abound for a trip for recovery.
The car is stuffed to capacity
Ready to move along from anticipation.

Suitcases filled with books
Not to mention a few clothes.
Nothing is left behind including
The various games to avoid boredom.

With a turn of a key, it grumbles
And with a puff of smoke, it rumbles
With another click it shifts into gear
And the silver bullet drives off with no fear.

Sun kissed with the lips of this wave.
The heat makes the passengers crack
Open a window to let wisps of cool air.
Fill the car with half-baked hopes of coolness.

Air conditioning may be present,
But the old man with a hole in his head
Claims it to be too much of a burden for
His wallet, fuller than our own to handle it.

Yet it seems to the innocent child
That the old man in front is simply another miser,
who cannot let go of few more bucks to the wind,
as the traveler approach the Coquihalla.

Something claws at the child's stomach.
Something stirred, something churned,
something turned, doing backflips.
Maybe it was the motion of the vehicle
snaking around the winding roads,
Or perhaps something he had eaten,
that disturbed the internal balance.

He just recalls having that banana
For whatever reason, it disturbs him within,
When combined with a long 3hr trip.
Darkness cloaks his eyes; he lies his head down.

Slowly now he levels his body
Hoping for a pit stop to breathe.
Finally they approach midway in Merritt,
where the comfort of Home Restaurant resides.

Mountainous Driving
(Okanagan abound)

———

Moving onward, moving forward.
The road that leads ahead
Bathed in the sun lit heat
Lies beyond some ways toward vacation.

In doing so, the key turned again.
Putt putt grumble rumble
Goes the silver bullet Chrysler,
just roaring to go forth.

All set to hit the road
after taking a deep breath
Clearing the head of all the fuzz.
The boy is now eager to driven on.

Snaking and winding around his eyes
meeting the clear glass frame
soaking in the movie reel of beauty.
Caught in awe-struck glamour.

In this height in elevation
these mountains blanketed with trees
with this vastness speaks greatness
in spite of the scars that show.

From previous fires long ago
that have taken a bite out of the forests.
Since the dry brush remained ever drier,
And so provided more fuel for later fires.

The old man in front began to fiddle
With the radio listening for road reports.
Hoping no ill-willed road blocks awaits
In front of our path between the mountains.

As the travelers move along
They come to approach the toll booth.
Other cars pass through like refugees
From another country trying to escape.

The old man in front rolls his window
Down to see the eyes of the gatekeeper.
Some cash was exchanged and we
Moved merrily freely to new territory.

Following a network of paved cement
The travelers move swiftly to their destination.
A city hidden in mountains, the valley opens
To a single bridge across a single large lake.

Cracked Skies

———

Away on a first grand adventure
Across the flat terrain of the homeland.
Heading straight toward some ominous
Black wispy clouds full of uncertainty.
Even after the last Timmy stop, the travelers continued.

Thinking with all hope that it was
Moving the other way but no
They were following them like some
Blood lusting shadows waiting to strike.
Seeing the lateness of the decision.

The wiser driver takes the wheel.
Time was chosen to tour another
Small forgettable old town
That the driver once lived in.
Strolling down memory lane.

Something rumbled in the deep.
The winds began to pick up
The dust like some loose hand
Tossing it around like a dirt salad.
Soon the Honda Odyssey moves on.

People now retreat indoors
After viewing this development.
Observing the signs, the peddle
Is pressed into the floor
And the travelers fly as if a fire is at their heels.

Stalagmite peaks begin to form
Out of the grey canvas that looms.
Next thing we knew the sky banged
And a streak of blue lightning touched
Down as the sound wave vibrates through the glass.

Unable to stop they continued
Through hoping with all hope
That their luck holds out
And the travelers are still able to dance
In between the strikes from the sky.

Tightening their grips in their leather,
the heart thumping beats of the raw
natural power of the blue cracks all around.
Even as the funneling clouds try to reach the travelers,
the driver presses onward.

Finally, it approaches them
The Best Western on the highway.
The skies flash with contempt
Signaling the pending warning.

Camp Amusement Park

Racing on, racing through
The Traffic, heavy with exhaust.
Here the travelers glance at the signs
Displaying the departing times at sea.

Never before scene with city-eyes
The glamourous sparkle of the ocean.
The gem of the west coast parts.
It is all soaked in and absorbed.

By the innocence of the young prisoner,
released for a time for experience
of a childhood all wish for.
Even ones trapped by the gov't for children.

All the other boys and girls arrive and gather
At the drop off zone ready to go.
All the bags and other things are given away.
To the truck taking our needs across.

Ushering the little kids, the herders
Guide them into the large boat
Also never experienced by the young Boy,
who is thrilled to be aboard.

Suddenly a loud drone sounds
Signaling this ferry's departing
Farwell to the other unfortunate
Souls, who could not arrive sooner.

Not expecting this ear-splitting moan.
His heart starts in a skipping beat.
His eyes open wide, now awake.
His ears clapped with protective hands.

Swaying side to side, the boat trudges on
Through the clashing waves that slap.
The sides of the metal bolted hull,
Carrying the several decks of cars.

Sweet salty scents of the ocean
Tides come freely in and out
Of the boy's clear nostrils
Grasping the unclogged breath outside.

Quickly, now wandering the halls
Of this vessel, mapping all the important rooms.
Inside the little eager head wondering,
What he should do first.

Discovering the cafeteria, he ensues
The cheeseburger deluxe combo
From BCs own personal Spot of White.
Finding a corner, he eats his morsel.

Too soon the boat slows down
And directs itself into the other harbour
With the locking of some gears.
All the children exit single file.

Guided and ushered on through
A line of buses awaits these campers.
Impatient as excited puppies out for a walk
Eager to get on toward this new experience.

Moving out in quick succession
The cheers and jeers of the others
Egg the bus drivers on, in order
To hurry to the exciting destination.

Annoyingly loud, the roar of the engine
Vibrates through the boy's fingertips and into his head
Making it impossible to think
Not to mention the grinding bumps.

As the road shifts from pavement
To rock embedded dirt roads.
After much recoil from the tire springs
Of the school bus, they all arrive at last.

A parade of councilors and other children
Come running to the arrival of some
Royal like persons as the party
Erupts for the newbies thirsty for fun.

Shortly they are chosen and selected
Into their new cabins, after which
All of their things are collected
And taken to their home for two weeks.

After much to do another gathering occurs.
A certain prayer is uttered, then the feast begins.
Getting to know one another
Proves to challenge the young boy.

Once all was consumed, all were dismissed
Back to the cabin allowing the feeling sink in.
All lie quietly playing cards
Among other kinds of board games.

The next bright day of camp,
yet another religious gathering
for another ritualistic manner
of Christian affairs for the children.

Brainwashed into entitlement the other kids follow loyally.
Dismissed away for scheduled fun.
Out on the oceanic canvas, a waterpark lies.

Deep with the forests that surround
the encampment we have a series
of complicated cables, some with chairs
others with climbing stones.

What to choose what to choose
Too many baffling choices
to be handled by the young one,
who has known only one... survive.

Running in the Wind

Bursting out of the mechanical doors
a man and his dog go running
through the breeze of a thousand
different flavours of flowery scents.
Thick with playful emotion.

Slipping through the long grasses
the two scamper on in the soft
marshlands that surround the rocky
terrain right under through the lane,
ever more playful they shall remain.

Playing the harps of much needed release.
Tightened strain is eased out of the pores
ever greater relaxed among the bushes and trees,
which tame the inner beast.
All the while our dog catches bees.

Smoke through Trees

Out on the outskirts of the city
caught in the middle surrounded on all sides.
Drier than the previous years it set
ablaze now transforming uncontrollably
into a heartless rage of consumed air.

Rising with no shape or form
the blackness chokes out the sunlight
and takes in all the comforts of home
and eradicates the security of our nature.
Many more flee for refuge far away.

Alerts are issued city-wide everywhere
so daunting, if one comes knocking.
Scarier still, if the flaming hand
comes reaching through the trees
to touch the dry brush lying on the shingles.

Blowing jet hot air on the demon
Flames hot blooded for more
consumption of the wooden structures.
Even hosing them seems to be dire
to the fighters loosing against it.

Blindly Walking

Slipping off into a wondrous land
allowing the soft skin press into
the ground with the pads of my feet.
Feeling the busy little critters
tap their little legs in and out of the toes.

A wisp of cool breeze comes down
to play with the clear minds
of a young child escaping reality
observing every little cotton ball
that drifts by aimlessly through the air.

Sliding his hands along the sappy bark of the moss
covered trees all around
seeing his clothes become sticky and
hot as he wipes his soiled hands
upon the grey slippery fabric shorts.

A Dance of Coloured Leaves

Holding on to dear things
only known to fear things
grasping at frail connections
never meant to stay attached
to the central branch of the trunk.

With nothing more than a gentle breeze
they break away from familiar ties
to an old wilted tree, incurable
of its imperfect cracks caused
by internal turmoil with beetles.

Gleefully riding the air currents
the bright oranges and yellows
release the senses of many other
loves of much deserved freedoms
after years of diseased attachment.

ABOUT THE AUTHOR

David Ferguson is an aspiring young author starting out on his writing career. His love for writing began in high school, mostly in his final year. He discovered a certain talent for it, when he began receiving praise from teachers and peers. Poetry more or less was an outlet for his horribly unstable past, being tossed around between different foster parents as his biological parents were unable to properly take care of him. Many of his poems stem from that past. Currently he working on novel called the Sixth World: Forgotten Children of Gildre Ample, which is a fantasy novel based on a place where he grew up.

Find out more about David at http://www.awalkofmanypaths.com/ or like me on Facebook.com/A Walk of Many Paths

One Last Thing...

If you enjoyed reading this book of poetry, I'd be very grateful if you'd post a short review on Amazon. Your support really does make a difference and I read all the reviews personally, so I can get your feedback and make this book even better.

If you'd like to leave a review then all you need to do is click the review link on this book's page on Amazon here http://amzn.to/1lDAUWE

Thanks again for your support!

Printed in the United States
By Bookmasters